# Geometries For Life

## New Era Sacred Geometry

*Dedicated to the Arceus*

*Louise Gallant*
*: Emmarose :*

Geometries For Life


Published by Tellwell Talent
Printed in Canada

ISBN: 978-0-2288-5868-3 (Paperback)
ISBN: 978-0-2288-5869-0 (Hardcover)
ISBN: 978-0-2288-5870-6 (Ebook)

Editor: Leanne Bolton
Front cover: Louise Gallant
Book Design and Geometries: Louise Gallant
Cover Geometry: Sacred Alchemy
Gratitude to the Radiant Rose Academy

Website: Lightlogos.com

Lightlogos Creations

# Table of Contents

# Foreword

Many climb mountains, relishing in breathtaking views. Others prefer exploring the deep seas and discovering fascinating new lifeforms. What makes one choose one path or another is for each one to discover. As for me, I have been interested in what happens inside our hearts and minds, in thoughts and feelings in the landscape within. There I discovered an inherent love for Art and Science. Art that moves the Spirit with kindness and inspiration, and Science that advances the well being of all.

It is through this lens that I witness today a flourishing number of artists, scientists, and thinkers also, that bring forth amazing art works, inventions and ideas. Their contribution is magnificent, and it fills me with great humility as I look at the multiplicity of what is coming forth. Each one is unique in style and expression, and offers enough variety to go around to fit all tastes. It is in that perspective that I present to you the Sacred Geometries, illustrations, that came through me. I am but the instrument.

The journey has been unfolding for many years and shall continue...

## Gratitude

In Truth, nothing is ever done alone. And without the encouragement, support and love of so many people, I could not have found my way. I am eternally grateful to all the individuals I have ever met on this path I walk.

What you will find in these pages is a collection of Sacred Geometries

What you will get from these pages... Depends on you

*Harmony*

*Picture :: keys :: Openings*

# Sacred Geometry

## This Grand Subject

The purpose of this book is not to give you a discourse on Sacred Geometry. There are many books and websites full of information on this very special subject. We have seen Sacred Geometries in many shapes and forms, generated, but not limited to, what we are familiar with such as the Fibonacci sequence, using Symmetry, Pi, the 5 Platonic solids, Fractal dimensions, and the list goes on. Those are tools one may use while in the creative process, and rightly so since they hint and reveal what a Masterpiece the Universe is.

In my own perspective and understanding, Sacred Geometry is definitely purposeful. Think of it as a Pattern associated to an Idea, and this pattern allows for the idea to reach the full potential in a manifested reality, faithful to its goal, intent, and accomplished in perfect Harmony.

An Idea generates a pattern

*Passion...*

## The Creation

An underlying 'grid' is always present in any Sacred Geometry, and harmony is at its core, allowing the unfoldment in perfect timing.

Sacred Geometry is 'abstract' and with this quality can bypass the intellect. If one is able to relax and gaze upon one, then one allows the imagery to do its job. No effort required, just allow... three minutes of magic.

Sacred Geometry unfolds and operates within the Universal Laws of Love and Light

*Unique*

# The Artist

*Geometrist*

Emmarose :: Louise Gallant

## Louise Gallant ~Emmarose

I have always loved both art and science ever since I was a little girl, and I still do today. I grew up and after two successful businesses under my belt, I asked myself “What is it that I like to draw? Or paint? What was in me that I liked so much?” The answer was shapes, forms, and symbols. Then I thought: “What would Gratitude, Victory or Collaboration look like in shapes and forms?” Little did I know that this very question would start me on a fabulous exploration of Sacred Geometry. There you have it in a nutshell! This journey in geometry is ongoing to this day.
:o)

Each Creation is Unique
In Expression and Purpose
As it is... for each one of us

## Why this Book?

I woke up one day and felt a prompting to gather all the Sacred Geometries I had thus far completed and present them together, hence this book. Doing this compilation, I felt, would allow anyone interested to easily scan through the images, rest their eyes on a Geometry of their choice for the purpose of a contemplation, or to simply allow for a pause in the very busy lives we all live.

*Memory*

So let's do the Journey of
embracing Uniqueness
with each other

With the help of Sacred
Geometry, let's turn the key

# The Arceus

## architects of the universe

### Who are They?

I first heard of the Arceus through my service (work) at the Radiant Rose Academy. They are known as the “Architects of the Universe”…and introduced the function and purpose of what is called Sacred Geometry.

Sacred Geometries speak to my heart, hence my dedication, and my journey in service to the Arceus.

It was said that we have lost the ability to see the patterned images that are instantly present with each thought one has. This ability will surely return as part of our evolution.

"Receiving the Sacred Geometry of some Truth, is the fastest way to get this Truth actualized in your life. Looking at a Geometry feeds it with your Source Energy, and it returns all Energy back into the world."
~Arcaseus

Inherent within each Geometry is its Original Intent, Destiny, Divine Plan, and the Perfect Unfoldment of its Purpose and Fulfillment.

Source knows no imperfection, thus cannot conceive any

Humans can...

*Arcaseus . Arcameus*

*Source: Radiant Rose Academy*

*the* ARCEUS

# POWER

All Sacred Geometries are powerful. However I have named this section 'Empowerment Geometries' to give space to very specific ones.

***Path Walkers, Travel Well!***

# Empowerment Geometries

# ENLIGHTENMENT

A Natural Evolution

# CREATIVITY

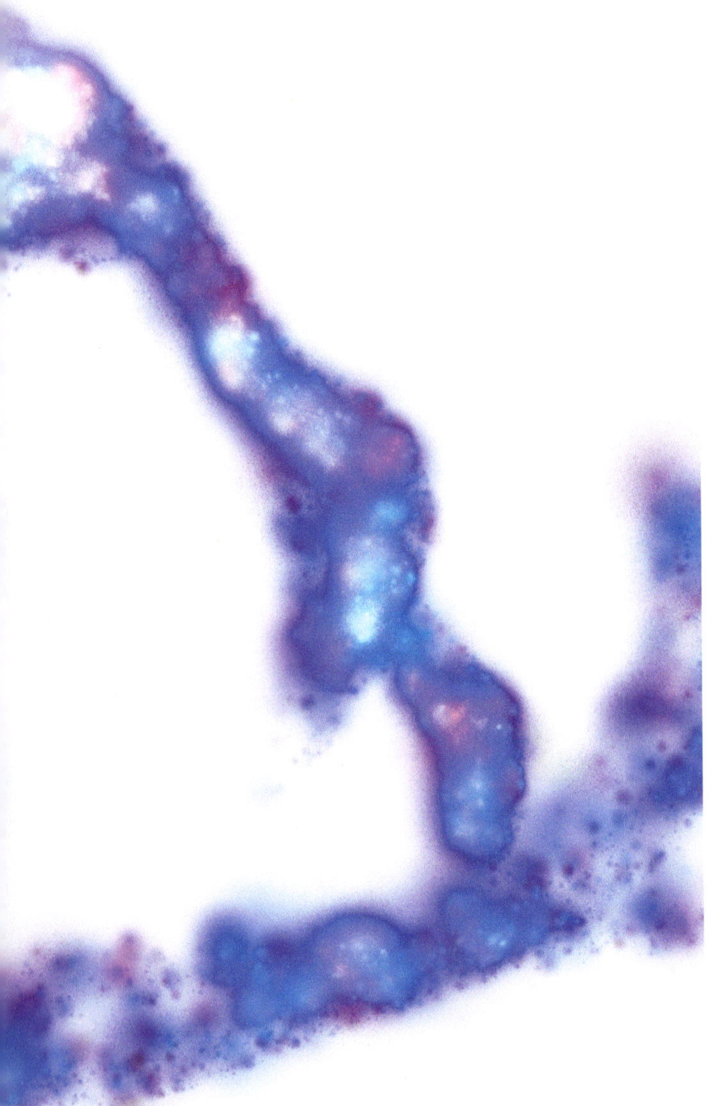

A Love Affair like no other
Fueled by inspired ideas
Rendered in Joyful activity
Expression manifested

Creativity

# HARMLESSNESS

Safe is my emanation

Openness is generated

The road is set

# METAMORPHOSIS

It seemed Life stood still for a moment...

A pause that lasted thousands of years

It took crisis.... but Time presents

A new 'Cycle'

Igniting changes

Inherent in the seed, within...

Ready for a Grand Metamorphosis

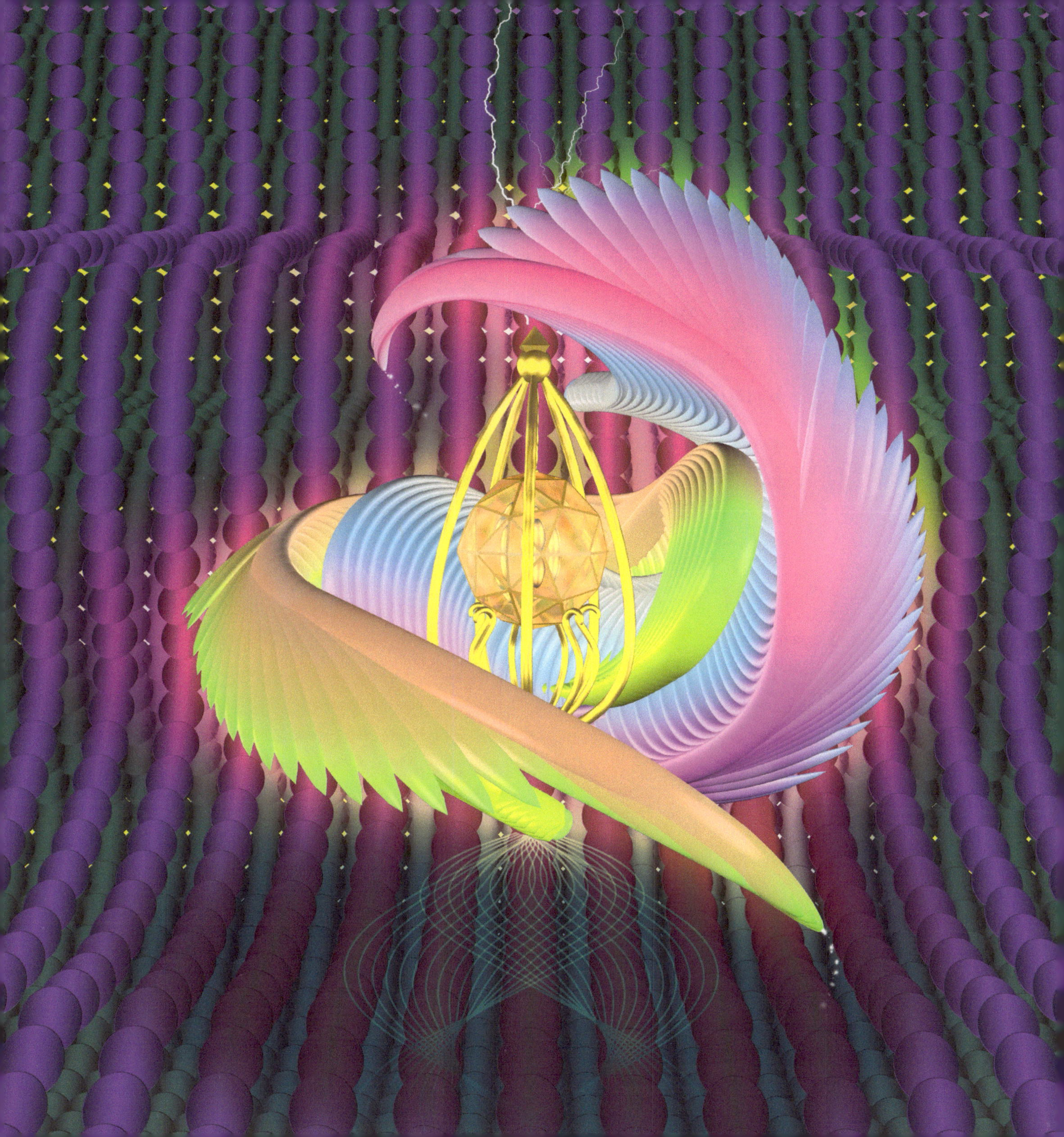

# VICTORY

It starts with the little things
It starts in small places

I stand Victorious on a day without Judgment
I stand Victorious in a day of Peace

# Golden Flame of Peace, Love, Purity and Happiness

A burst of Light in my heart
A burst of Light in yours

A feeling of Peace explores possibilities
Windows open, Happiness flows through

In greater Purity of mind
In greater Purity of body

Living in Appreciation

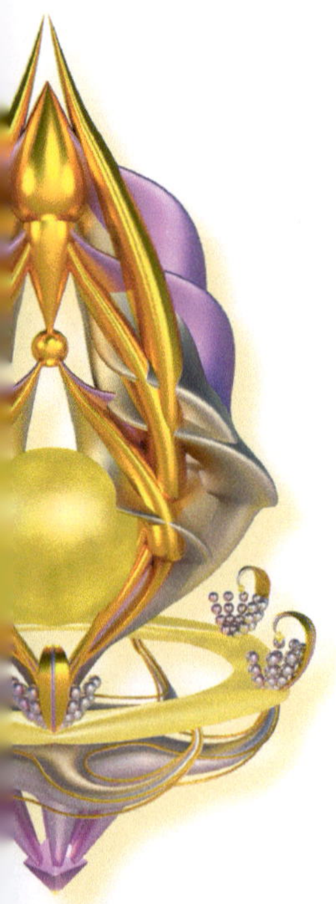

# MAGDALENE FORCE

I recall a power and strength
That moves celestial bodies

My eyes cast upon you,
I send you an invitation
and welcome your reply

# GOLD

How valuable you are!

You attract our attention...
for more reasons than people know

Not all is understood of your nature

Your true gift will shine within us

~

One day soon

# SILVER

How valuable you are!

More than we know at this moment

One day will reveal

the power of Your Attraction

~

A Love affair with Gold
On equal terms

# FROM HERE TO THERE

Form this point forward to somewhere Greater

There is always a place to go to
A place to transform into

What I choose is up to me
What I see and experience
Depends on me

~

Here, could be now
Now can already be the future
In my mind

# Transitional Geometries

# Cosmic Neutralizer of Disease

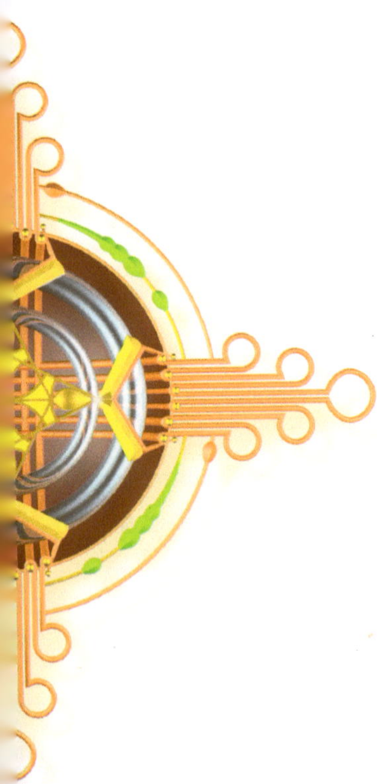

As I cast my eyes upon you...

Anchor in me the remembrance
of Truth

Health is my true nature
Forgiveness is my road to right alignment

I will use what you provide
and heal falsehood

# Cosmic Neutralizer of Consciousness of Lack

As I cast my eyes upon you...

Anchor in me the remembrance
of the One Law, that Law being Love

Abundance is not just for the few
It depends not on one river.

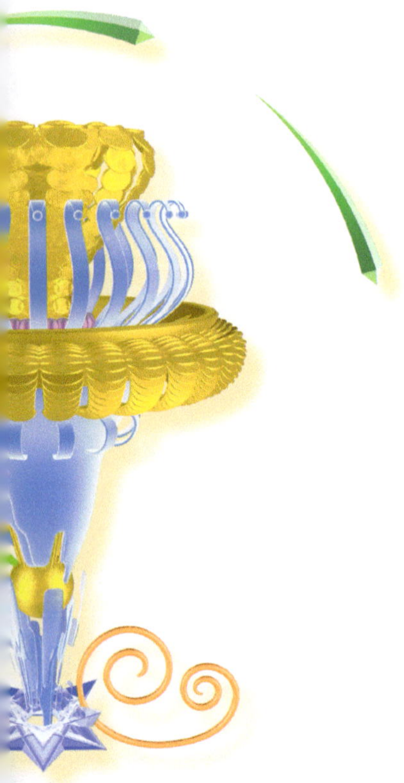

The ocean carves many streams
Unlimited channels of Richness
Richness of friends, support, supplies,
and so much more

Never shall I do without
Never shall I go without

# Cosmic Neutralizer of the Source of Unhappiness

As I cast my eyes upon you...

Anchor memories of Innocence
Dissolve false beliefs

Layer a peaceful knowing
A Courage to accept and surrender.

What I experience can be changed
Changeable as breath itself

Happiness! Take control!

# COMMUNITY

They gather on your surface

You teach them what you can

Some listen well

Others are still learning

One day the class will graduate!

# Countries, Cities Geometries

# India

## Luminosity

## IN ALL

# Canada

## Justice

## FOR ALL

# Ireland

## Willful DETERMINATION

# United Kingdom

## Union

## UNDER GRACE

# New York

## Opportunity FOR ALL

# USA

## Liberty FOR ALL

Alabama
Alaska
Arizona
Arkansas
California
Colorado
Connecticut*
Delaware*
Florida
Georgia*
Hawaii
Idaho
Illinois
Indiana
Iowa
Kansas
Kentucky
Louisiana
Maine
Maryland*
Massachusetts*
Michigan
Minnesota
Mississippi
Missouri
Montana
Nebraska
Nevada
New Hampshire*
New Jersey*
New Mexico
New York*
North Carolina*
North Dakota
Ohio
Oklahoma
Oregon
Pennsylvania*
Rhode Island*
South Carolina*
South Dakota
Tennessee
Texas
Utah
Vermont
Virginia*
Washington
West Virginia
Wisconsin
Wyoming

*Original 13 Colonies

United States of America — UNITED States of America — United States of AMERICA — UNITED States of AMERICA

# States of the USA Geometries

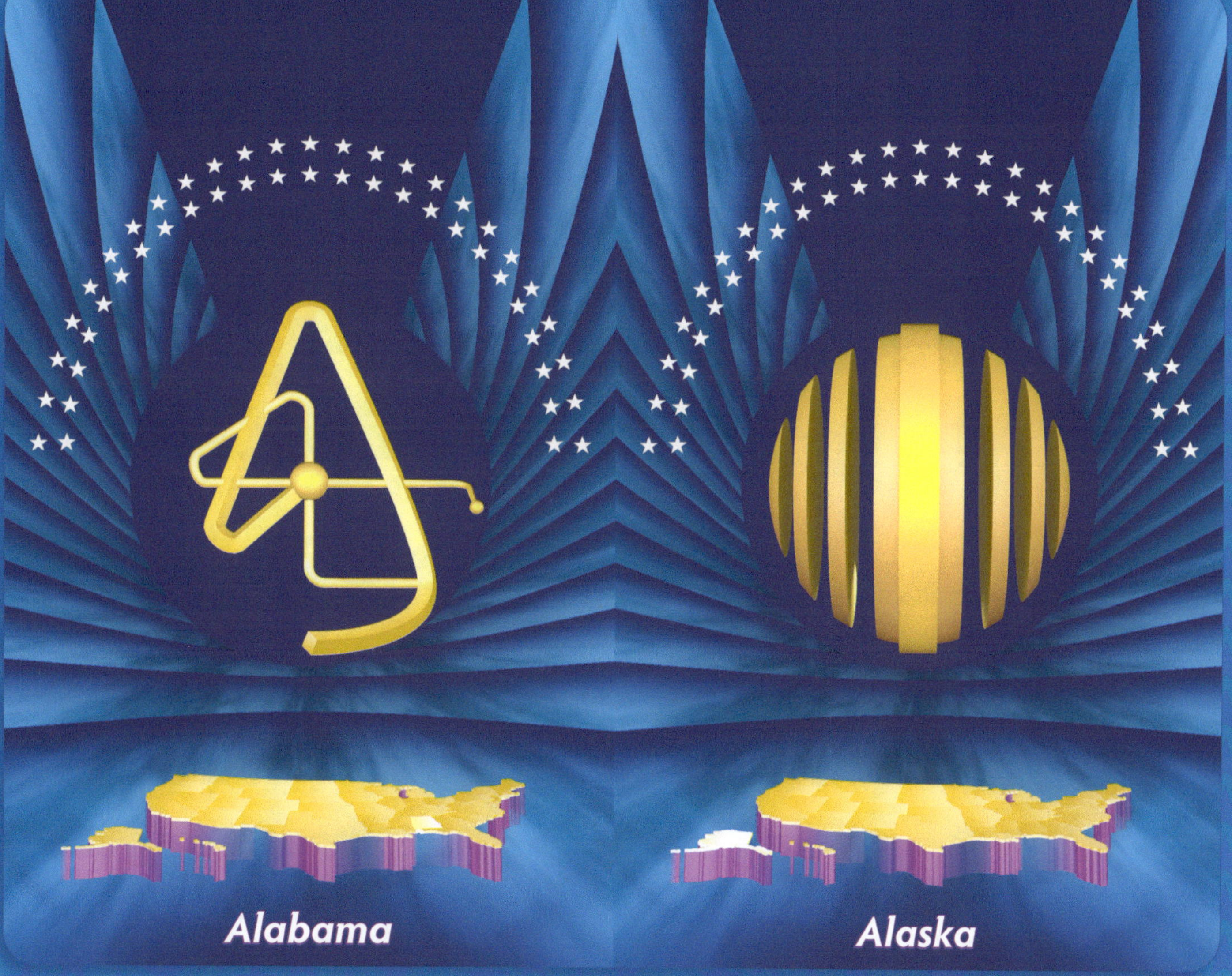
Alabama
Alaska

Arizona
Arkansas

California
Colorado

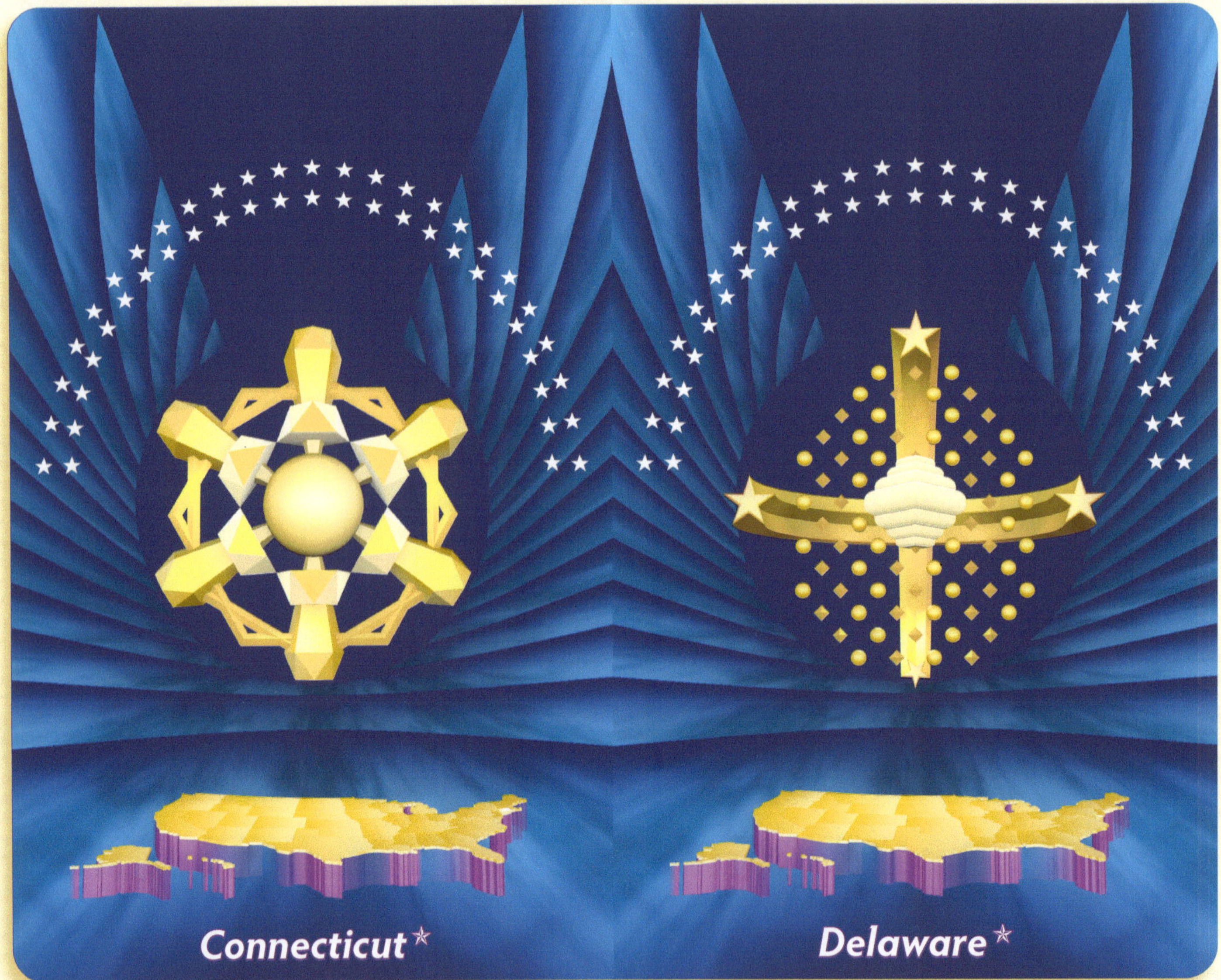


* Part of the original 13 Colonies

* Part of the original 13 Colonies

Hawaii
Idaho

Illinois
Indiana

Iowa
Kansas

Kentucky

Louisiana

*Part of the original 13 Colonies*

* Part of the original 13 Colonies

Minnesota
Mississippi

Missouri

Montana

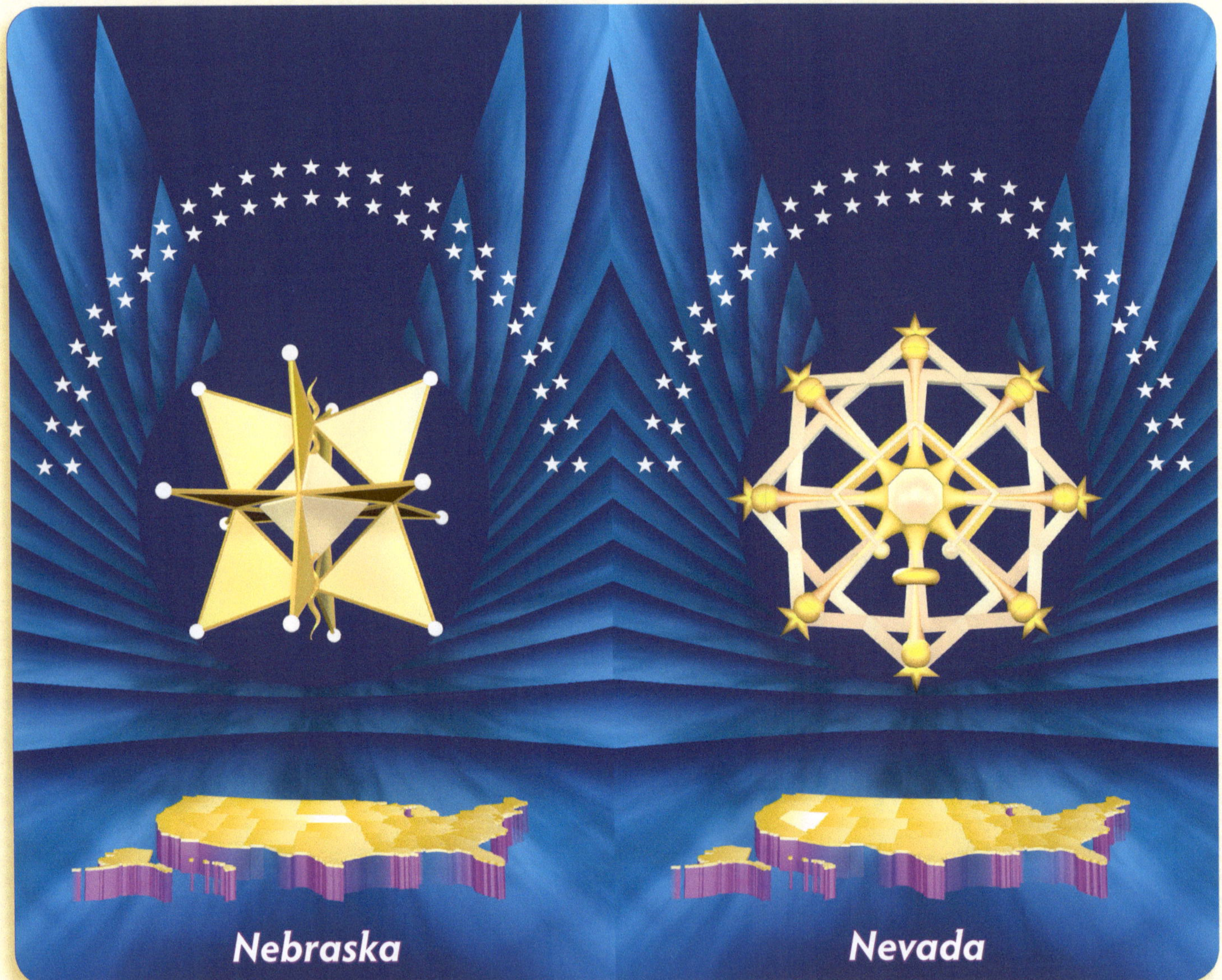
Nebraska
Nevada

* Part of the original 13 Colonies

* Part of the original 13 Colonies

* Part of the original 13 Colonies

Ohio
Oklahoma

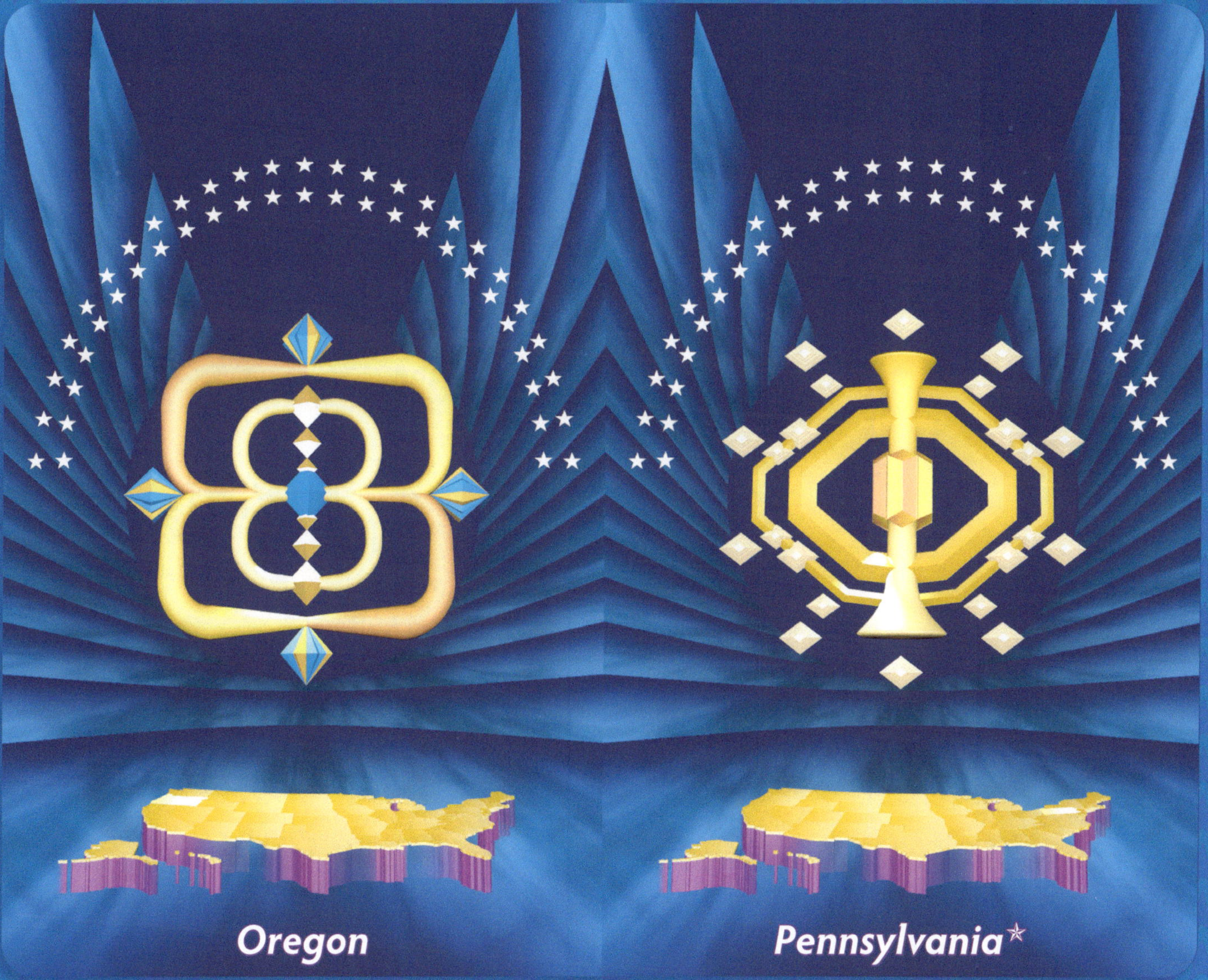


* Part of the original 13 Colonies

* Part of the original 13 Colonies

South Dakota
Tennessee

Texas
Utah

* Part of the original 13 Colonies

Washington
West Virginia

Wisconsin
Wyoming

Guardians of the Land,
we honour you

# May your uniqueness touch our hearts

*Apache*
*Cherokee*
*Cheyenne*
*Choctaw*
*Comanche*
*Crow*
*Navajo*
*Paiute*
*Pawnee*
*Shawnee*
*Shoshone*
*Sioux*

You were here, long ago... Original Tribes, walking on this territory called the United States of America.

You kept it as pristine as you could for Its destiny to unfold

# Original Tribes Geometries

Apache
Cherokee

Cheyenne
Choctaw

Comanche
Crow

Navajo

Paiute

Pawnee
Shawnee

Shoshone
Sioux

12 Manifestation
1 Light
2 Love
3 Mind
4 Heart
5 Soul
6 Immortality
7 Omniscience
8 Omnipresence
9 Omnipotence
10 Will
11 Creative Expression
Sacred Oracle of Delphi

# Oracle of Truth Geometries

# KNOWER OF ALL TRUTH

Matters not what you say
Truth is Truth

Truth springs Eternal
Matters not the season

Matters not the disguise you paint upon it
Its Timeless Rivers come now
Its flow unveils all
It clears your eyes of all mirages
Just wait for it, it will come

~

Truth lies outside of 'good'
Truth lies outside of 'bad'
Outside of 'for' or 'against'
Outside of 'possible' or 'impossible'

Truth lives in you in all its beauty
It can dance you in infinite Joy
Allow it to be

# Light

Electric in Nature

Conception

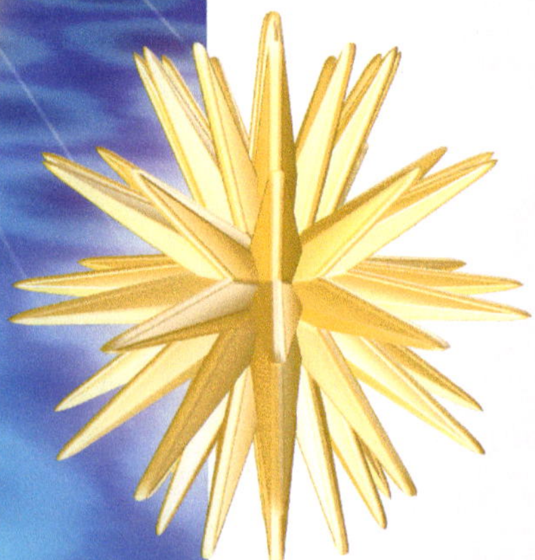

# Love

Magnetic in nature

Fulfillment

# Mind

A Real Mind

Dances with Heart

# Heart

Rhythm Generator

Dances with Mind

# Soul

Each breath

A power of Renewal

# Immortality

Source

In Perpetual existence

# Omniscience

All Knowing

Inherent and True

# Omnipresence

My Reach

Everywhere

# Omnipotence

All Power Available

Always

# Will

Impact of results

Intensity measured…

# Creative Expression

Unstoppable

Inherent within each heart

# Manifestation

Natural result

Befitting Universal Laws

# A Door to Everything

***Intermission -|-***

I cast my eyes upon you

The strength of your Love Emanates,
and shatters the wall
I had unknowingly built
between us

In this revelation
My gratitude expands,
Inundates and dissolves any particles
touched by imperfection

The Kingdom rejoices

This illustration is included as
a reminder to open doors.

# Sacred Oracles of the Divine Mothers

## Oracle: Becoming What You Love

May this be an Inspiration

*Content Source: Radiant Rose Academy*

# Divine Mothers Geometries

# Oracle of the Queen Mother Akasha

I AM a Being of Cause
. Divine Love .

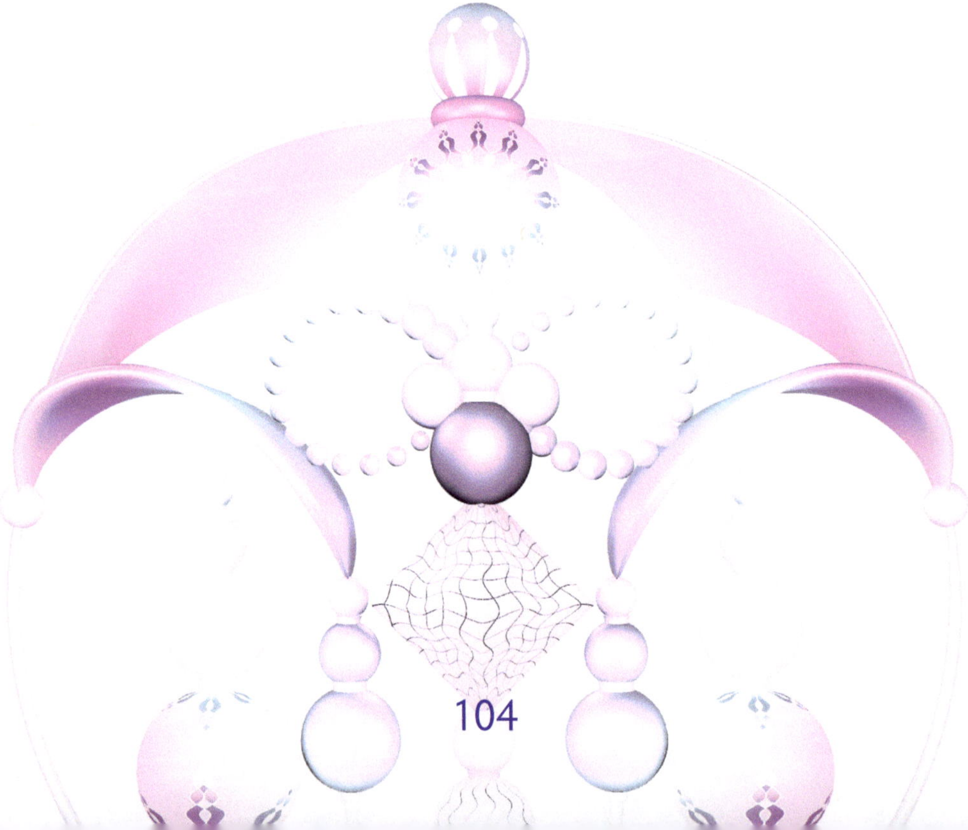

# Oracle of the Queen Mother of Light

I AM Light
. My reach is Infinite .

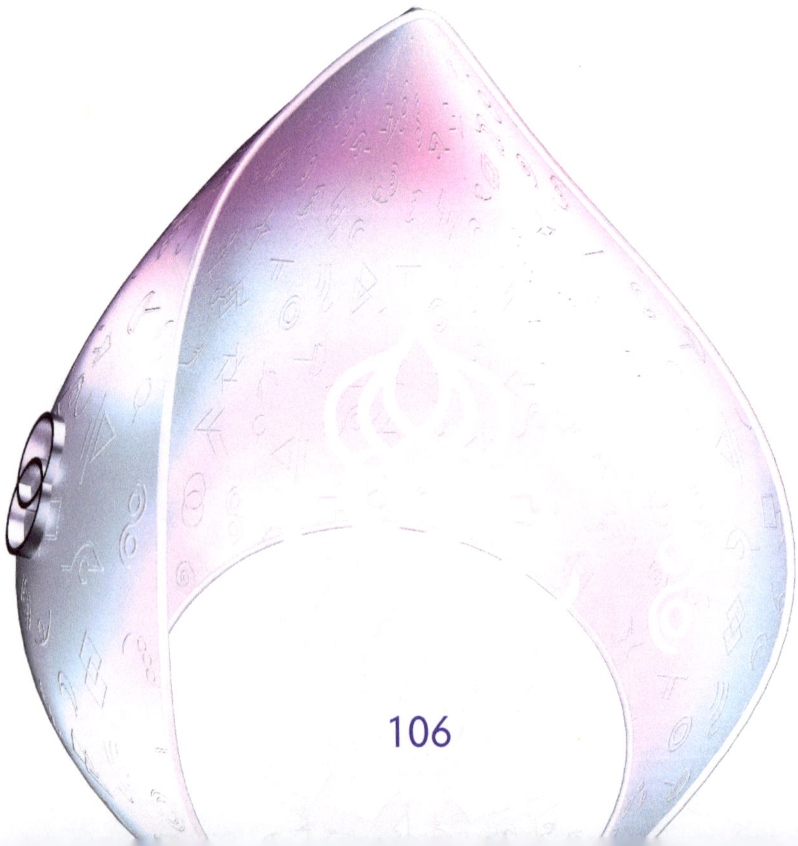

# Oracle of the Queen Mother of Jupiter

I AM manifestation through Vision
. Manifested .

# ORACLE OF MOTHER GODDESS OF VENUS

I AM Love
. To your System of Worlds .

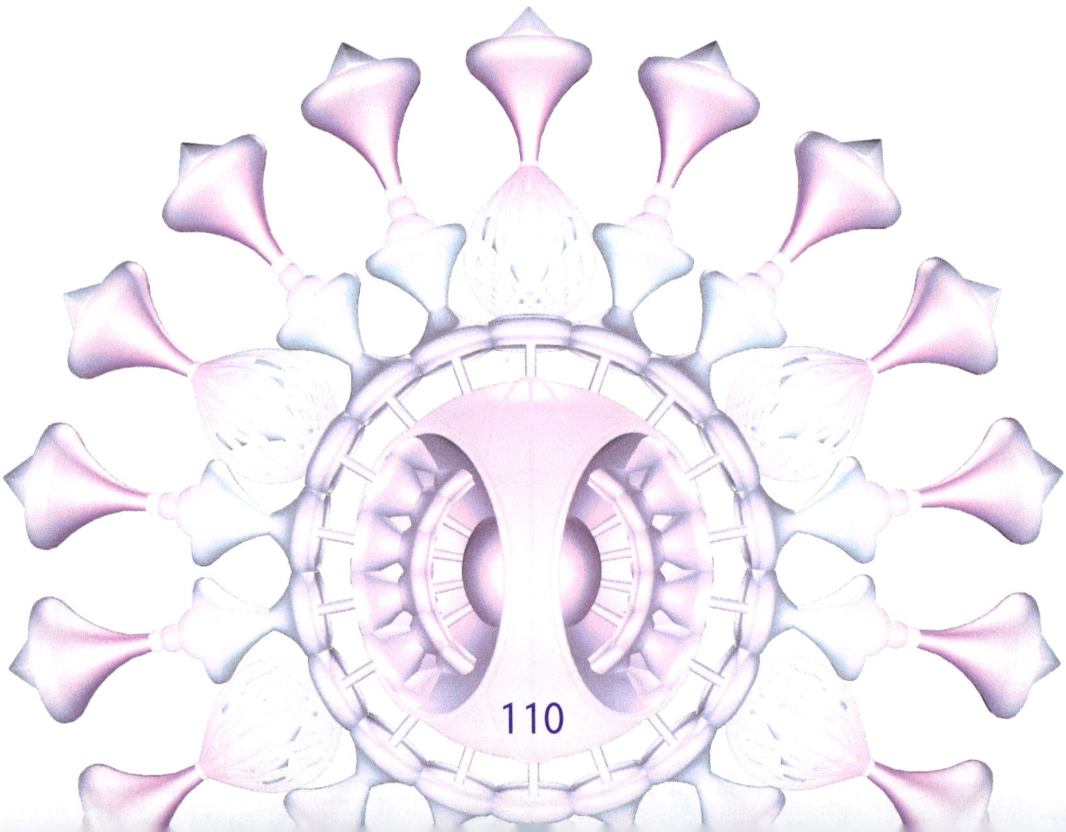

# Oracle of Mother Mary

I AM Intelligent Love
. Everywhere .

# Oracle of Grandmother Anna

I AM Wisdom
. Wisdom for all Ages to come .

# Oracle of Mother Nada

I AM Inspiration
. Driving Force of Inspiration .

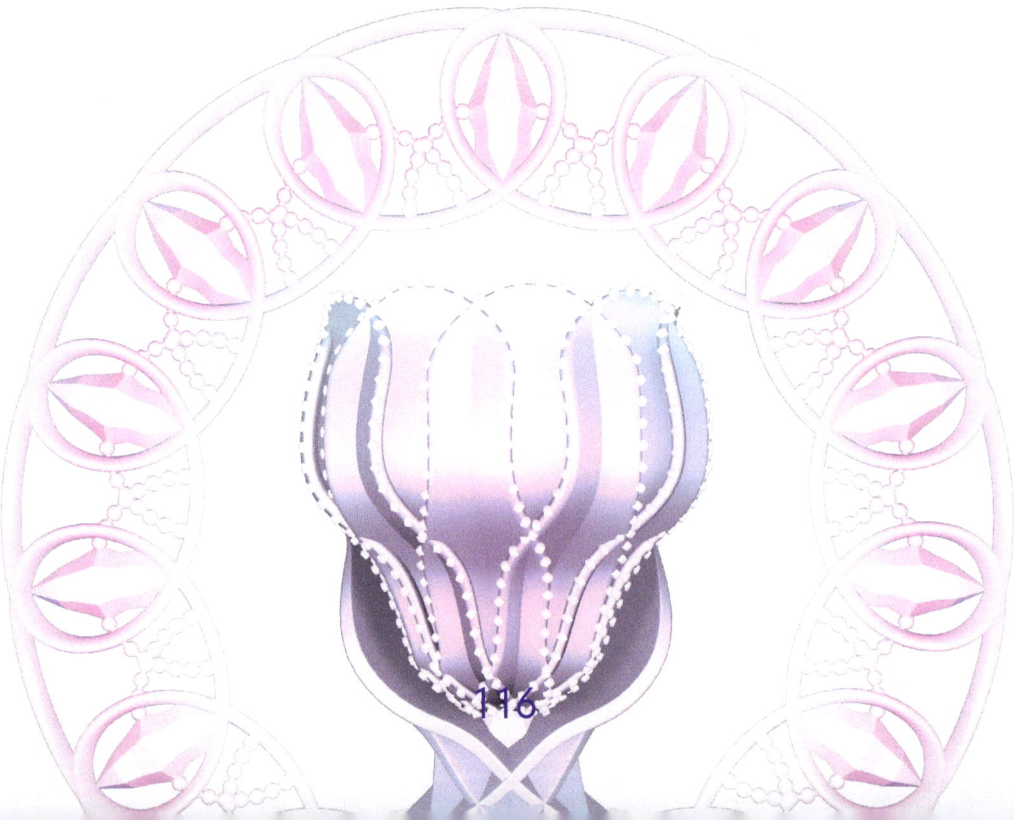

# ORACLE OF MOTHER META

I AM Shadowless Light
. Everlasting Shine .

# Oracle of Mother Vesta

## I AM in Divine Partnership with ALL
## . Sacred Union .

I AM the Force

. Perfect Outcome .

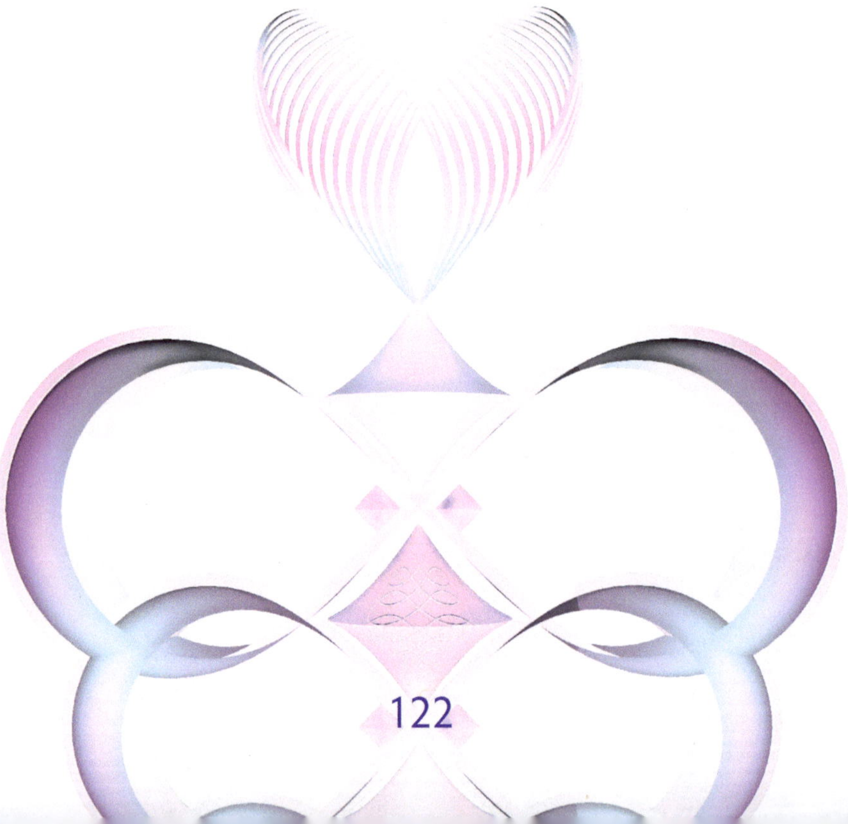

# SACRED CHALICES

## Chalices of the Goddesses

# Sacred Chalices Geometries

# PEACE

I choose and drink Peace

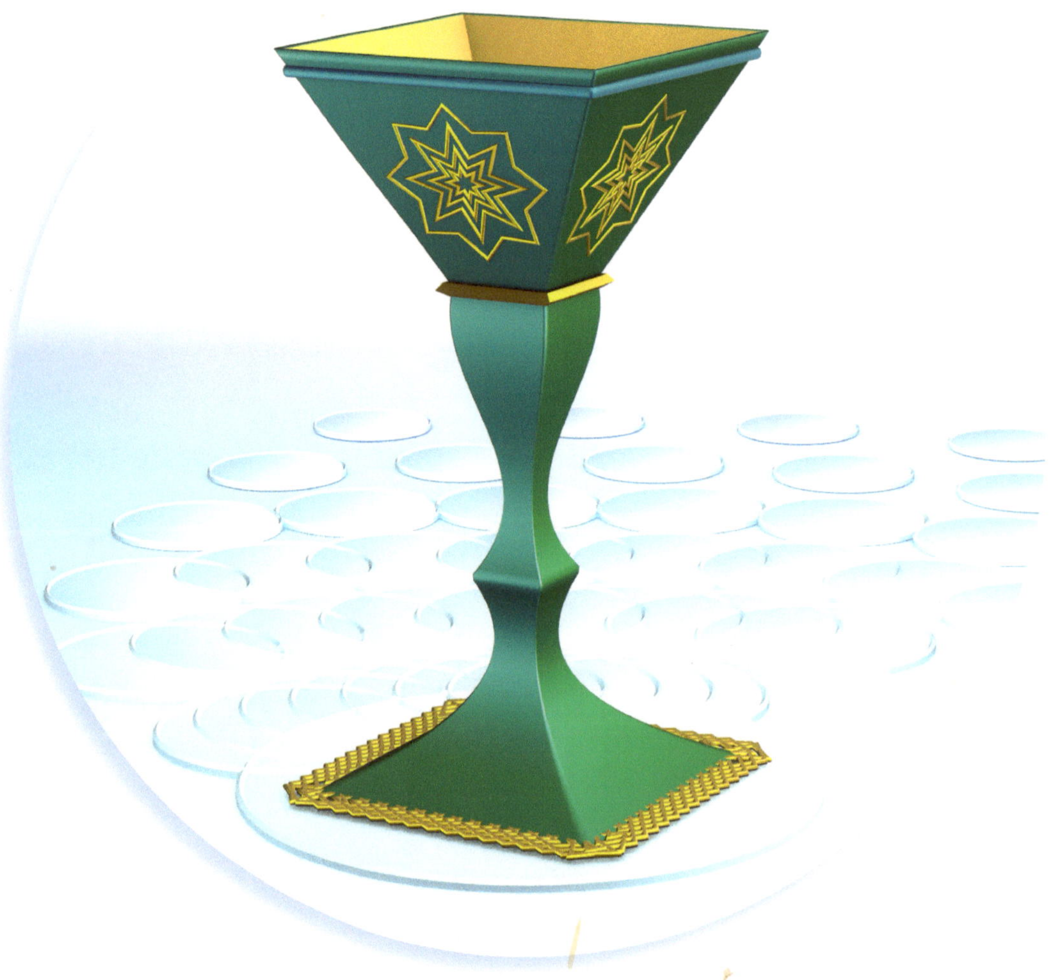

# PURITY

Pure in thoughts, feelings, and body

# LIBERTY

Liberty, innate to Life itself

# HARMONY

Harmony keeps the balance

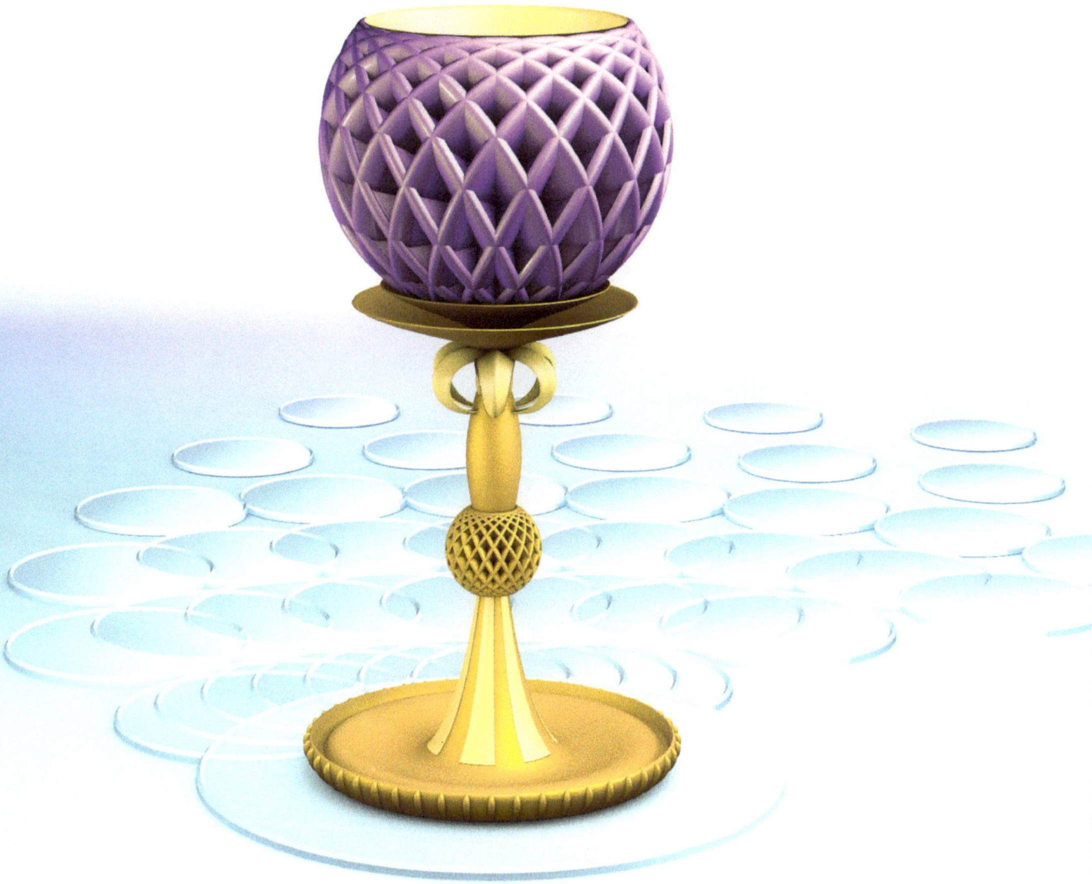

# JUSTICE

Justice in Equality and Understanding

# VICTORY

Visioning Victory one moment at a time

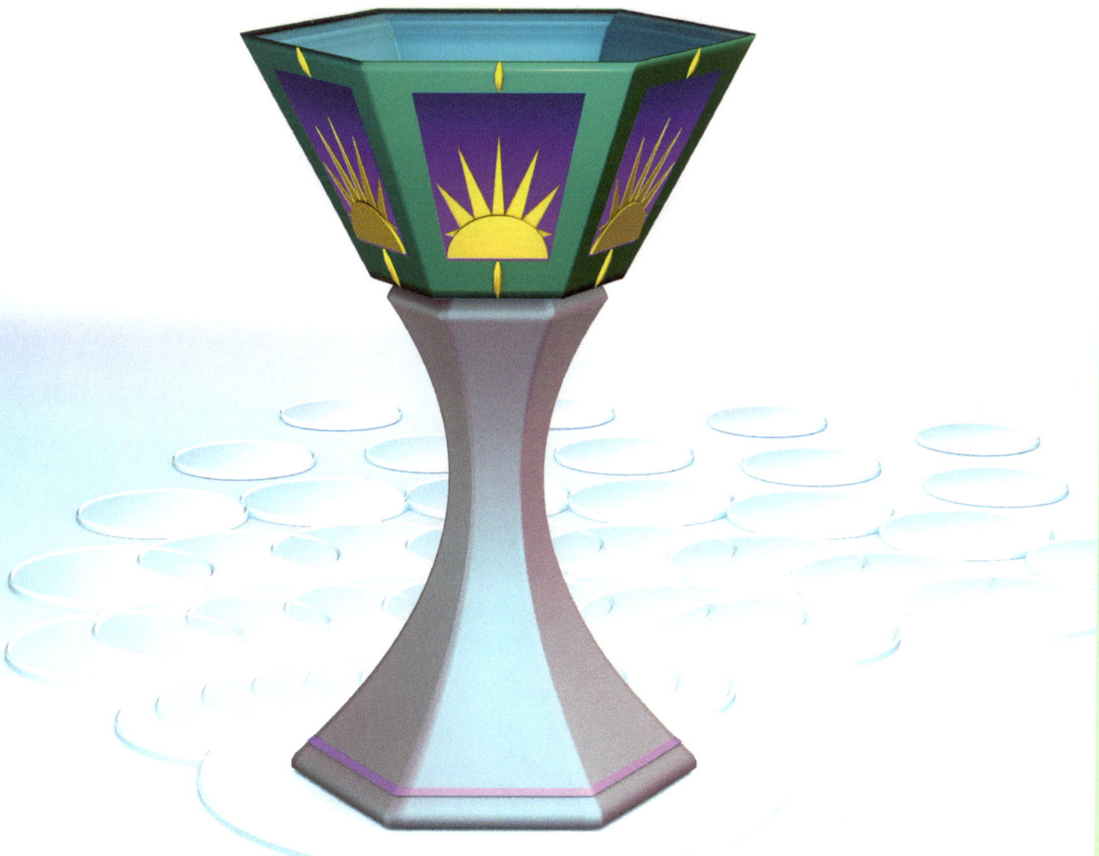

# HOPE

Hope magnetizing all that is required

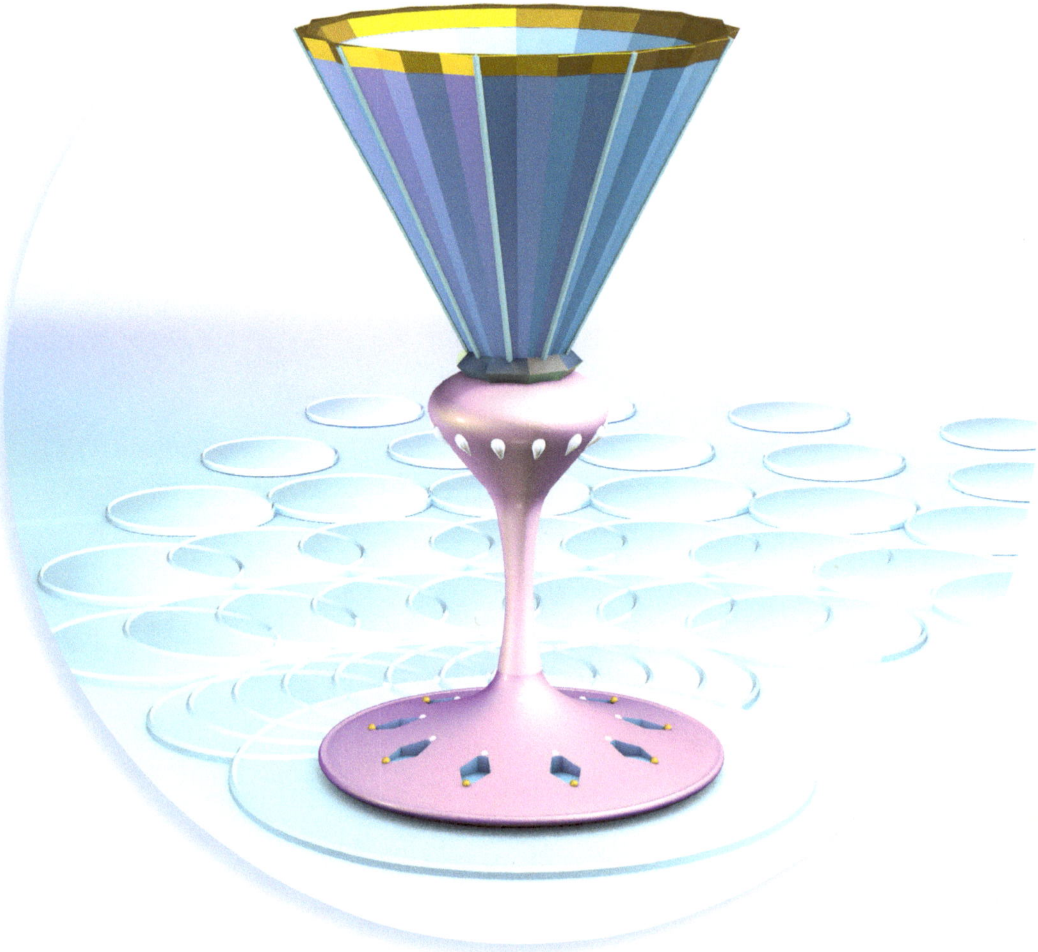

# FAITH

I stay the course

# LOVE

Love in All things, for All

# LIGHT

**Illuminates All Paths**

# UNITY

A dance in Equilibrium

# MUSIC

Music of the Universe, Beauty beyond imagination

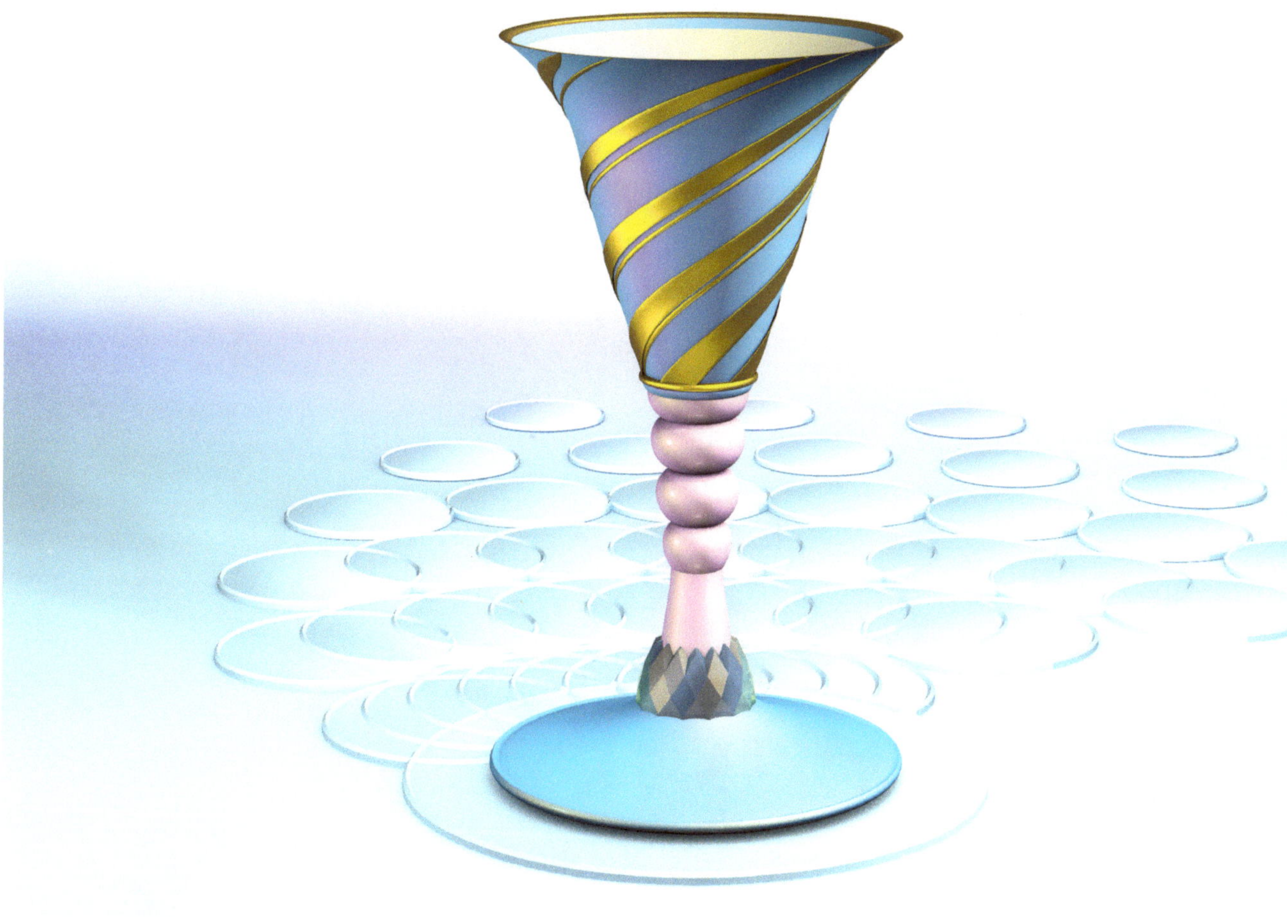

# CHARITY

Pure unwavering Joy

# RESURRECTION

## ...the rise

### 1 to 33

Resurrection! A raising activity
up and out of limitations.

A Journey from Duality to Polarity.
Light and Love dancing in harmony.

An evolutionary, developmental process.

# Resurrection Geometries

# Akasha

## 1

Cultivating and readying the Fields of our Consciousness by expanding Knowledge and Use of the Sacred Flames of God; Universal Heart and Soul

1

*Source: Radiant Rose Academy*

*'God' refers to Source, which gives Life, Is Life.*

# Achrista

## 2

Planting the Seeds of
Resurrection within the
Garden of our Consciousness;
Initiating the Rites of
Passage of Resurrection,
The River Jordan, Baptism

2 Achrista

*Source: Radiant Rose Academy*

# Atlanta

3

The Nature of Mind to accept
and govern ideas of Evolution.
As Creators we begin the
efficient use of understanding
and enlightening our minds

3

Atlanta

*Source: Radiant Rose Academy*

# Alectra

4

Cosmic Intervention to begin receiving the Electronic Patterns of the Untouchables; Recognition and cooperation with the Elemental and Angelic Beings to assist process

4

Alectra

*Source: Radiant Rose Academy*

# Amaya

5

The Choice between
human and Divine natures,
contrasting experience is
complete; opening the way
for allowing the completion
of Balanced Source Ego

5

Amaya

*Source: Radiant Rose Academy*

# Abulana

6

The Christ Release of Light
into the mind; The Heart Flame
expands love in our feelings as
our expanding Consciousness
begins collapsing the
imposed boundaries of
mind and feelings

6 Abulana

*Source: Radiant Rose Academy*

*'Christ' refers to a state of Consciousness*

# Amedata

7

The Light of Divine Mind
passes through a Sacred
Nerve into the Heart as we
begin practiced meditation
to train the mind to receive
the Light of the Christ

7 Amedata

*Source: Radiant Rose Academy*

# Asaylona

8

First Actualization of the Tree of Life Teachings that include the Law of Love, the Outpouring of Love and Blessings, and the Temple of the Most High

8 Asaylona

*Source: Radiant Rose Academy*

# Alleluia

9

Revelation of the Ascended Master Mystical Valleys are revealed for Meditation: Emanuel's Valley of Lilies, Master Germain's Valley of Violets, and Akasha's Valley of Roses

9 Alleluia

*Source: Radiant Rose Academy*

# Atona

10

The Sacred Fire offers Transformation, Transmutation, and Transfiguration; The first phase of Sacred Fire Breath and the Sacred Flames for Transformation of the physical garment

10

Atona

*Source: Radiant Rose Academy*

# Adisponiata

11

Receiving the Ascended Master
Gifts of Intervention planned
for the Seventh Golden Age;
The Planetary Logos reveal
Dispensations for this age



*Source: Radiant Rose Academy*

# Amiracala

12

The Electronic Miracle Mantles
unfold around us as the
Heart Flame Lantern of Light
begins to govern the Physical
Garment; The Golden Cross
appears above the Lantern

12

Amiracala

*Source: Radiant Rose Academy*

# Aluminata

13

Waves of Cosmic Light begin to intensify as they flow through the mind opening new centres of brain activity; Pineal and Pituitary Glands activate

13

Aluminata

*Source: Radiant Rose Academy*

# Asunata

14

Through receptivity, focus and meditation, the Omniscient Centre of Consciousness can be glimpsed and experienced; Expanding shifts of awareness occur

14

Asunata

*Source: Radiant Rose Academy*

# Allegra

15

Consciousness of time,
space, and distance changes
as the Individualized I AM
Christ Presence expresses
out from the Centre of
our Consciousness

15

Allegra

*Source: Radiant Rose Academy*

# Abraviona

16

Resurrection of the Heart
First Elemental Beings aligns
Elements of the physical
body with mind that is
receiving expanded Light
Impulses of the Christ

16

Abraviona

*Source: Radiant Rose Academy*

# Apreneecia

17

I AM Rose Presence takes control of the Will of the Feeling Body; Currents of Electronic Energy quicken the speed and rotation of the Feeling Side of Life

17

Apreneecia

*Source: Radiant Rose Academy*

# Adanteamora

18

Magical Words and Phrases express the full activity of their meaning and intention, as created and used by each Creator Being; Introduction to Divine Magic begins

18

Adanteamora

*Source: Radiant Rose Academy*

# Aroseaya

19

Every Breath is sacred, every
Breath is unique, no two
Breaths are the same; Spiritual
Breath is practiced and
perfected; the Breath of Life,
gift of the Divine Feminine

19 Aroseaya

*Source: Radiant Rose Academy*

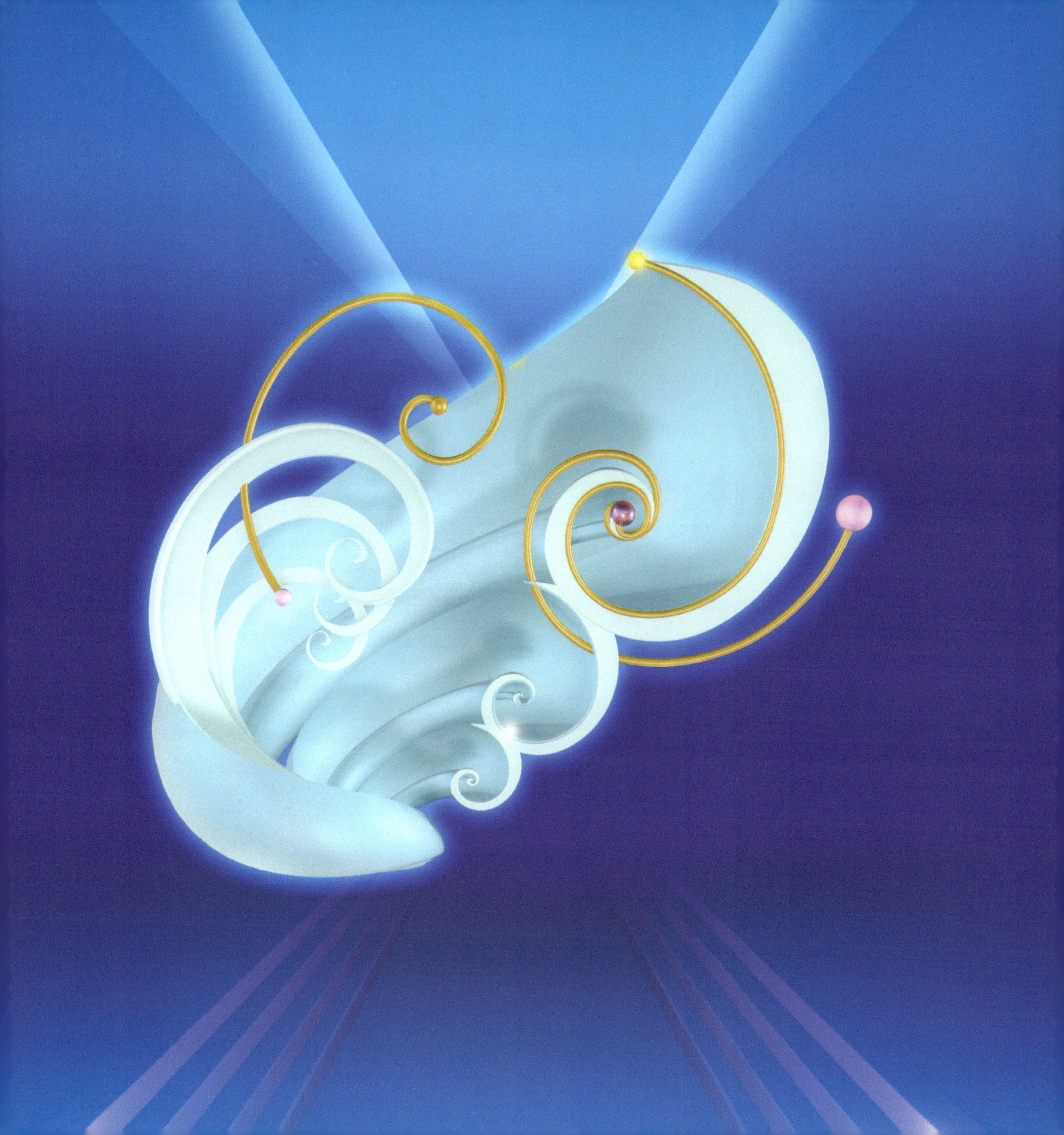

# Akujamonteya

20

The Soul stirs and readies to
greet the Initiate; Relationship
between the Heart and
the Soul fully restored; the
Door to Everything begins
to open ever so slightly

20

Akujamonteya

*Source: Radiant Rose Academy*

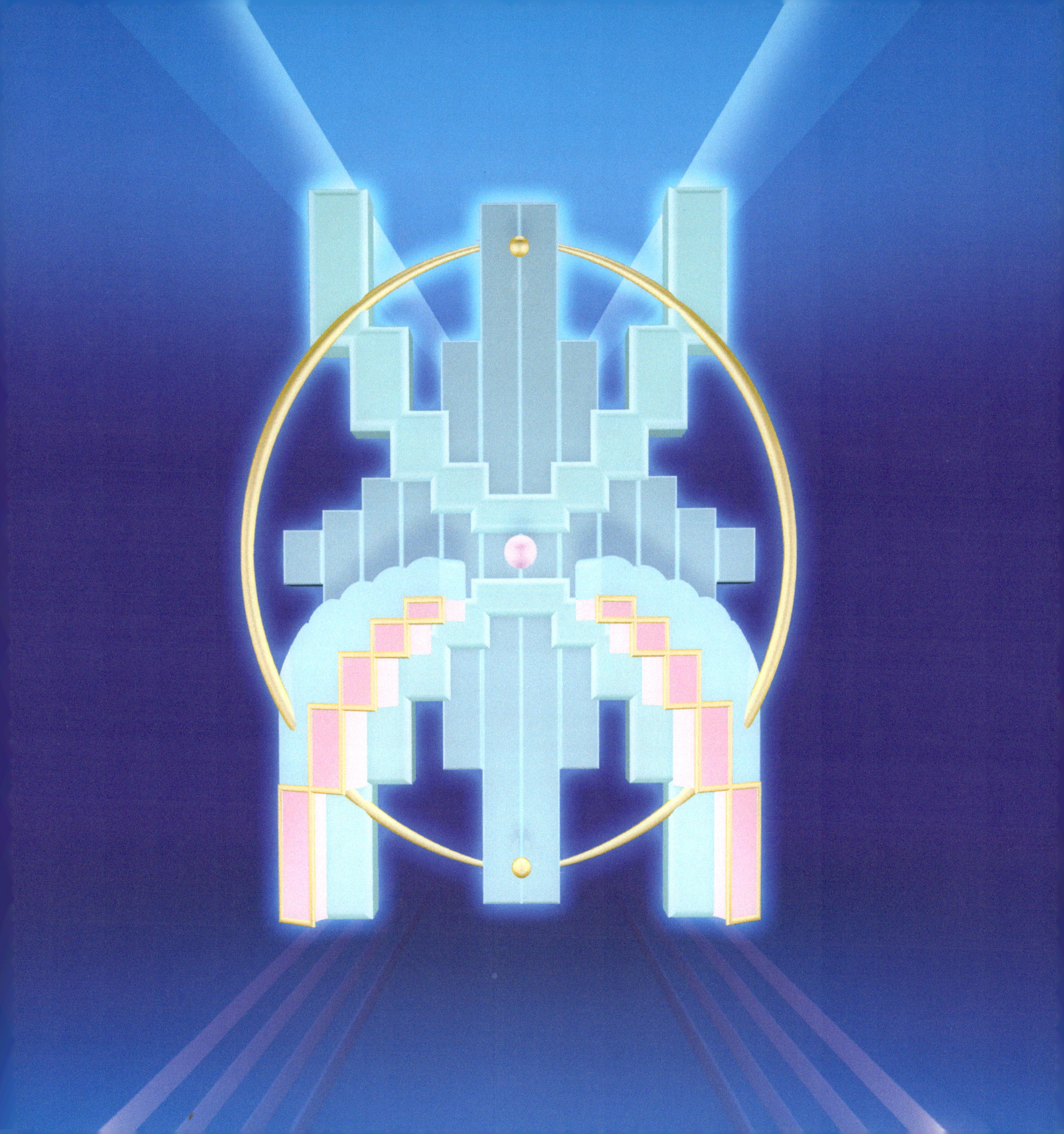

# Annamaria

## 21

The Sacred Mothers come
to prepare us to enter into
the Temple of God at the
Centre of our Consciousness;
Divine Escort by the
Mother's Presence occurs;
Regeneration, Renewal,
and Resurrection begins

21 Annamaria

*Source: Radiant Rose Academy*

# Avasilencia

22

The Initiate has perfected the Activity of entering the Great Silence for Prayer and Meditation; Contact with the I AM Christ Presence occurs; The experience of 'Where I AM, God Is' unfolds

22 Avasilencia

*Source: Radiant Rose Academy*

# Alementa

## 23

All Elements of the
physical body united by the
Resurrected First Element,
become extensions of Mind
imbued with Truth, Love,
and Wisdom; Feeling Body
unifies Mind and Physical
Body as one and the same

23

Alementa

*Source: Radiant Rose Academy*

# Aloahfiora

24

Creator Eloah Plumes in our heart nurture the experience of Oneness with Divine Mother Presence of the Universe; Our Consciousness begins to surge through the Flower of Life Blueprint

24 Aloahfiora

*Source: Radiant Rose Academy*

# Afelohima

25

Creator Elohim Flames
in our brain nurture the
experience of Oneness with
Divine Father Presence of
Universe; Our Consciousness
begins to expand through
the Flower of Life Blueprint

25

Afelohima

*Source: Radiant Rose Academy*

# Atominachia

26

The Atomic nature of our physical bodies become open and sensitized to the Electronic Pressure of Cosmic Light Substance; the Point of Light in the centre of each cell expands fulfilling physical embodiment

26

Atominachia

*Source: Radiant Rose Academy*

# Arasunprescia

27

A Golden Aura of our Inner
Golden Sun's Presence forms
around the upper half of
our physical embodiment;
Rays of Light from within
pour out into the world

27

Arasunprescia

*Source: Radiant Rose Academy*

# Asymphonia

28

Our inner hearing is elevated
and attuned to the Music
of the Higher Spheres; Our
faculties are perfected by the
Incoming Christ Mind; The
Musical Symphony of the
Universe reveals instantaneous
time, space, and travel

28

Asymphonia

*Source: Radiant Rose Academy*

# Achristalibera

29

The Christ is liberated in each of us; The crucifixion of Consciousness comes to an end; Our Higher Mind becomes one with our daily thinking mind

29

Achristalibera

*Source: Radiant Rose Academy*

# Aclavisaurea

## 30

The Golden Key is given;
Meaningful understanding and
comprehension of all hidden
truths is provided; The Key to
all Conclaves and Invitation to
all Ascended Master Gatherings

30

Aclavisaurea

*Source: Radiant Rose Academy*

# Aconcordiaveritata

## 31

We become Divinely
Harmonized with all Universal
Truth and Beingness;
Harmonized with One
Presence, One Power, One Life;
God realized and actualized
in all living form and matter

31 Aconcordiaveritata

*Source: Radiant Rose Academy*

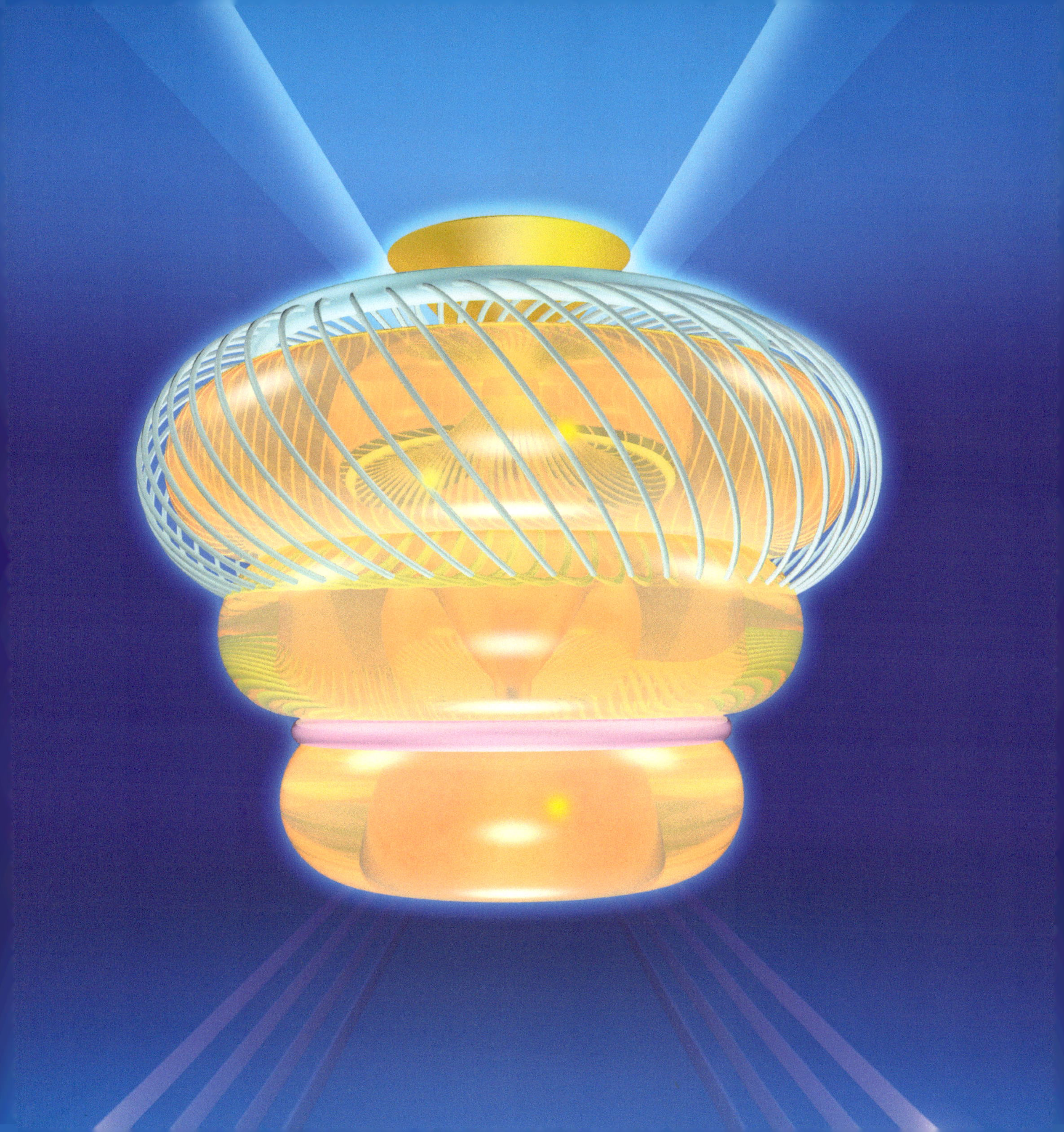

# Aconsumata

32

It is done; The Divine Union of our Earthly Embodiment with our Higher Christ Consciousness; The Journey Home is complete; Return to the Father/Mother's House, the Sun of all Suns; Full Resurrection is achieved

32 Aconsumata

*Source: Radiant Rose Academy*

# Achristamessia

33

As Christed Beings on Earth,
the Messiah Consciousness
emerges within each of
us; Advocacy of the Christ
takes place on Earth; Divine
Fulfillment of Seventh
Golden Age unfolds

33

Achristamessia

*Source: Radiant Rose Academy*

# METATRON'S CUBE

## To BE

***A Choice, Age of Pisces***

## To Become

***Age of Aquarius***

CPSIA information can be obtained
at www.ICGtesting.com
Printed in the USA
LVHW070457111121
703047LV00002B/4